Taykon Books

The Ultimate Speed-Reading Book

Read Fast AND Remember -
Learn how in less than 20 Minutes

Kick Butt in the Information Age!

Taykon Books

This edition first published in Great Britain by Taykon
Books, 2003

Taykon Books: The Post House, Barracloughs Lane,
Barton-Upon-Humber, North Lincolnshire, DN18 5BB

A CIP catalogue record for this book is available from the
British Library (from January 2004)

ISBN 0-9545692-0-2

Printed and Bound by: Pardy and Son, Parkside,
Ringwood, Hampshire, BH24 3SF, United Kingdom

Edited by: Morris Taylor

Cover Illustration: Tania Konstant
http://www.taniakonstant.co.uk

Also by Tina Konstant

Successful Speed-reading in a Week, Hodder and Stoughton, 2000 (ISBN 0-340-84950-9)

Teach yourself Speed-reading, Hodder and Stoughton, 2000 (ISBN 0-340-78094-0)

Mental Space (Co-author Morris Taylor), Pearson, 2002 (ISBN 1843040166)

For
☐ More on speed-reading
☐ Information about future titles by the author
☐ Further information about the author
visit:

http://www.tinakonstant.com

Acknowledgments

Thanks to the students who, over the years, attended the courses and helped condense this material into a precise piece of information.

Thanks also to Alex Pattison and Jim Anderson and the staff at Angus Council who reviewed the book. Also thanks to Eric Summers and M-C McInally and the students at Webster's High School in Kirriemuir, Scotland.

Additionally, thanks to Kate Pirie and Mandy Whyman who acted as idea sounding boards; to Penny Thompkins and James Lawley who have been there and done that: they helped me avoid some of the bigger mistakes I might have made in pulling this project together.

Also thanks to Tania Konstant for her illustrative brilliance over the years: http://www.taniakonstant.co.uk

And special thanks to Morris Taylor - Editor.

In less than 20 Minutes, learn how you can

- [ ] **Find** information quickly

- [ ] Make studying **easy**

- [ ] Read non-fiction material **faster**

- [ ] **Remember** technical and complex material

- [ ] **Clear** clutter in minutes

- [ ] **Process** a 200-page book in less than 60 minutes

- [ ] **Apply** what you read

- [ ] Read **smart**

- [ ] Read with **purpose**

CONTENTS

CONTENTS

Introduction

The aim of this book is to help you to manage information in a way that will make thinking easier, life better and you richer.

Speed-reading, as the term implies, is about reading fast. But there is more to it: for new information to have any value, you need to retain, integrate and apply it.

You might have questions such as:

- "What is the fastest possible reading speed?"
- "How do I remember what I read - when I need to remember it?"
- "How do I maintain concentration when reading technical or scientific material?"

> **!**
>
> The key to fast and effective reading is having a reason to read.

☐ "Is speed-reading easy to learn?"

If there is a limit on the speed at which people can read, we don't yet know what it is. The world-record holder for speed-reading can read a book the size of "War and Peace" in less than 20 minutes and retain enough to answer questions on it.

The ability to retain and recall is the most relevant outcome of reading. If you do not intend to remember what you read, why read it?

Easy to Learn

The effective reading system (described in Part 1) works just by using the five-step process. Follow the guidelines and you can learn to manage new information fast and efficiently.

> **!**
> The ability to retain, recall and use new information is as important as being able to read it quickly.

5 Steps to Easy Information Management

The five-step system will help you:

- ☐ Explore reading material using at least three different methods.
- ☐ Find information relevant to you without missing out what is important.
- ☐ Find information you require quickly.
- ☐ Integrate new information with what you already know.
- ☐ Accurately recall new information when you need it.
- ☐ Manage volumes of non-fiction information confidently and easily.
- ☐ Read and retain new information when under pressure.

> **!**
>
> When you understand what you read. It's much easier to remember it.

Become familiar with the five-step system outlined in Part 1. Then adapt it: combine or omit steps to suit your purpose and adjust it to the particular style of non-fiction such as newspapers, articles, memos, books or magazines.

PART 1

The Five-step Effective Reading System

It works!

It is easier to remember something if you understand it and are familiar with terminology, themes, concepts or jargon.

The purpose of the 5 Step System is to ensure that you:

1. Understand, retain and recall information by becoming familiar with structure, content, language and concepts.
2. Find exactly what you need without having to read irrelevant or unnecessary material.

The over-riding rule in effective reading:

Always know why you are reading something:

What is your PURPOSE?

3. Never miss relevant information.

Depending on the depth of information you want, steps one to four of the system described below could take between five and 50 minutes for a book of about 200 pages. The time for step five will depend on the *amount* of information you want.

Step 1: Prepare

Preparation should take no more than five minutes.

Lack of focus interferes with concentration. It frustrates reading. Preparation helps you focus. Your aim in *preparing* is to highlight areas that you want to study and to ~~exclude~~ what is unnecessary for your purpose.

> **!**
>
> When you know what information you are looking for you will find it. If you do not establish purpose, you will only notice what stands out.

To establish your purpose and

prepare ask yourself these questions:

1. What do you already *know* about the subject?
2. What do you *need* to know: is it general information or is it the answer to a specific question?
3. How and when do you intend to *use* the new information? Is it an essay, exam or report? General interest? A presentation? When? Next week, next month, next year, or do you need it in 10 minutes?

Step 2: Structure

Over-view the material to familiarise yourself with the structure:

- ☐ What does it look like?
- ☐ How is it organised?
- ☐ Are there summaries or conclusions?

☐ Is the book mainly words?
☐ Are there pictures?
☐ What is the print size?
☐ Is the information organised in sections?
☐ Is it a series of paragraphs?
☐ Are there bullet points?

Depending on your purpose, an over-view of the structure of a 200-page book or document should take between one and 10 minutes.

During Step 2:

☐ Read the front and back covers, the inside flaps, the table of contents and the index.
☐ Scan the bibliography.
☐ Determine the structure of the book: chapter headings, sub-headings, pictures, graphs, cartoons and images.
☐ Mark the parts of the book

that you are sure you will *not* need.

☐ Highlight areas you will need.

☐ Re-affirm your decision: What do you want from the book?

If it does not contain what you need, put the book away. You will save hours of work.

Step 3: Language

In steps one and two, you prepared yourself and studied the structure of the book. Now familiarise yourself with the language. Is there jargon? Is the language complicated? What do the acronyms mean? It should take five to 10 minutes to become familiar with the language of a 200-page book.

☐ Depending on the page size, scan at about a page

every two seconds.
- ☐ Highlight words linked to your purpose.
- ☐ Study the language: Is it technical? Non-technical? User-friendly? Are you familiar with it?
- ☐ Do you need a dictionary?
- ☐ Note the meaning of acronyms.

The speed at which you read is determined by your familiarity with the language. Try to recognise recurring themes or concepts during this step.

Highlight points relevant to your purpose.

Look up key words and concepts before you begin Step 4.

Step 4: Content

Most well-written material outlines the main element of a chapter in the first paragraph.

Similarly, the main idea of each paragraph is usually in the first sentence. So read:

- ☐ The first paragraph of every chapter and section
- ☐ The first sentence of every paragraph. If the paragraph is long, read the last sentence.
- ☐ Summaries or conclusions.

The more thoroughly you highlight, underline, circle, take notes and mind-map as you read, the easier step five will be.

Step 5: Selection

By the time you reach Step five you will have:

- ☐ Determined your purpose
- ☐ Studied the outline and the structure of the material
- ☐ Read introductions, summaries, and conclusions.

> **!**
>
> The more selective and purposeful you are about what you read, the faster and easier it will be.

☐ Become familiar with language, themes and general contents.

☐ Identified sections that contain the information you require

Now that you are familiar with the book, you simply need to *select* exactly what you need or want to read from the sections that are relevant to *you*.

And now, learn how to read it fast …

PART 2

Read more words Faster!

The Voice in your Head
Most people read at about 150 to 300 words per minute. And here's why:

As you read this paragraph, do you hear your own voice in your head "saying" the words you read? If you do, then you are reading to yourself. This happens because of how you were taught to read. It is the reason why you read at approximately the same speed that you speak. It's that simple.

Before you learned to read, you learned to recognise one letter or sound at a time. When you mastered that, you progressed to recognising one word at a time. You read out

> **!**
> Most people read only as fast as they can speak.

loud. That enabled your teacher to check that you recognised and pronounced the words accurately.

Then, instead of reading out loud to yourself, you read silently. You spoke to yourself. That led to a belief that you have to hear every word to comprehend what you read. You don't! Your "inner voice" became a habit. That's what we're about to change.

You could say that you learned to read with your ears instead of your eyes.

At first you were still learning to recognise the words. "Reading to yourself" was slow. As your vocabulary increased, you recognised words more quickly. Your reading rate increased until it stabilised at the number of words per minute at which you

> ***!***
>
> Most people use exactly the same reading strategies they learned when they were six years old.

speak. **But your reading *strategy* did not change.**

The aim is to help you change that strategy: to change the old belief that you have to read with your ears.

Read with your Eyes

To increase your "word-per-minute" reading rate you must accelerate your reading speed until you *eliminate the old habit* of sounding out the words in your head (often referred to as sub-vocalisation).

Two methods for achieving this are:

The guide

Place a guide (pen, pencil, or finger) underneath the first or second word of a line.

☐ Move the guide smoothly across the page from the

beginning of a line to the end of that line.

☐ Repeat on each line.
☐ Move the guide a little faster than is comfortable.
☐ The movement needs to be smooth and swift.

If you pause the guide, you are following your eye instead of *leading* it. If you sub-vocalise, your speed will not increase. When the guide moves quickly and smoothly, your eyes are forced to follow. Your reading rate will increase. The faster you move the guide, the less you will sub-vocalise. Your inner voice will be unable to keep up. The aim is to eliminate the old habit of reading one word at a time and to stop your attention wandering.

Speed-reading is a skill. It is easy to learn. Developing that skill does not mean you have

---

!

Using a guide will:
1. Focus attention
2. Prevent distraction
3. Increase your reading speed

---

to read fast all the time. Technical content, print size, mood, familiarity with the subject material and your purpose can affect reading speed. The ability to read quickly allows you to choose how fast or slow you want to read.

Selective reading
When you read information on a familiar subject and you don't want to miss important items in the text, use this technique.

- ☐ Read the first sentence of the paragraph
- ☐ Skim the rest of the paragraph for key words, and then, only if you think it necessary,
- ☐ Read the last sentence of the paragraph.

PART 3

Remember
what you read

The basis of Memory - Focused Attention

You will not remember what you read unless you pay attention.

Attention:

- ☐ Is **dynamic.** Focus on one thing only. Notice how long it is before your mind wanders.
- ☐ Has to be **undivided.** Try listening to more than one conversation at a time. You will hear bits of each, but you are unlikely to absorb either fully
- ☐ Follows **interest.** Boredom extinguishes attention
- ☐ Is maintained by a series

!

Focus and
Concentration
= Memory and Recall

---

of **discoveries**, new ideas
and insights

There are several categories of
attention:

Voluntary - When you voluntarily pay attention to something you do so naturally.
When you are totally absorbed
you are not easily distracted
and you don't have to force
yourself to concentrate.

Involuntary - When you carry
out routine tasks; for example,
driving: have you ever arrived
at your destination and not
been able to recall the journey
until later?

Dispersed - too many simulta-
neous activities or lack of
interest can cause a sense that
"everything attracts your
attention at once".

Aim to improve your ability to

> **!**
>
> **Purpose** =
> Focus and
> Concentration =
> Memory and Recall

focus your attention voluntarily and to focus attention fully even in situations where it once was difficult to concentrate.

The more interested you are in what you are doing, the easier it is to **concentrate** on it. Can you remember when you were last so engrossed that you lost awareness of time? Nothing distracted your attention. You were interested and motivated towards a goal.

Concentration increases when you have:
1. **Goals** - you know what you want.
2. **Motivation** - you know why you want it.
3. **Interest** - it facinates you.

If reading material is boring, or if it is hard to find motivation, take deliberate action:

- ☐ Close your eyes for a moment.
- ☐ Breathe deeply and take a little time to become still.
- ☐ Gather your thoughts and ask yourself what your purpose is.
- ☐ Write down your reasons for reading the material.
- ☐ How long do you estimate it will take?
- ☐ What is challenging about the information? What is easy?
- ☐ How will you apply what you learn?
- ☐ How will you benefit?

If your mind drifts, focus your attention. If you speak out loud as you write your plan, your concentration will improve and your desire to complete the task will take over.

Unless you intend to remember what you read, no matter how fast you read, you will have wasted your time.

Concentration

Without concentration, retention and recall is almost impossible.

Do you ever daydream? Gaze through the classroom window ... contemplate the wall as your computer screen flickers at the edge of your awareness ... drift somewhere pleasant as someone talks to you? Your eyes glaze. Absorbed in your thoughts.

When you daydream, you focus. You concentrate. You are absorbed to the exclusion of everything else.

Therefore, if you can daydream, you can concentrate. Learn how to apply it!

> *!*
>
> Daydreaming requires absolute focused attention.

Top 3 Memory Boosters

It will be much easier to remember what you read if you:

1. **Have a purpose:** Always have a reason for reading something.

2. **Use new information:** Explain. Discuss. Write. Construct arguments for and against. Think. Apply.

3. **Think ahead:** Think about when you intend to use the information. The method you use to understand, retain and apply it will vary depending on why and when you will use new information. If you are reading complex information, the method you use will differ from the method you would use if you only need a general understanding of it.

Memory techniques

Use techniques that give you the fastest reading speed and the best recall. Examples are:

Linear:

Make notes as you read or after each section. Add your own thoughts, ideas and cross-references. The more you include your own ideas, the more reliable your long-term memory is likely to be.

Key words:

Highlight words that carry the message. If you make separate notes, avoid making a key-word listing that makes no sense when you review it later.

Margin reading:

A book communicates ideas. Take ownership. <u>Underline</u>, circle, and highlight essential areas. Add and compare your thoughts to the author's. Do you agree or disagree? Note your reasoning. Highlight what you do understand. Underline what you don't understand then highlight it later when you understand it.

Do this *only* with books that belong to you. Or use "post-it" notes. The aim is to "interact" with the text.

Mind-maps*:

☐ Place the primary idea in the centre of a horizontal page.

☐ Secondary ideas form thick branches from the centre.

☐ Tertiary ideas flow from secondary ideas. And so on until you reach the finest detail.

☐ Use colour and symbols.

☐ One word or idea per line
(*For more on Mind-maps, read Tony Buzan's "*The Mind Map Book*")

> **!**
>
> The best memory techniques ensures integration of new and old information.

PART 4

Improve
Speed and Memory

These exercises help improve memory and increase speed.

Memory Stretch

Read one page as fast as you can, using a guide. Stop. Summarise what you remember. Read five to ten pages like this every day. Gradually increase the number of pages before you check your recall. Start with a familiar subject. As your ability and confidence increase, attempt more challenging material.

Speed Stretch
The "One Minute Trip":

☐ Read for one minute.
Count how many lines you have read.

☐ Read for another minute. This time read two lines more.

☐ Then read four lines more. Then six more. Then eight more. Then 10 more and so on.

As you practice and your concentration improves, stretch the One Minute Trip to two minutes then four then six then eight minutes ... and so on.

Always read for good comprehension and recall. As soon as you sense that you are unlikely to remember what you read, stay at that speed until you feel comfortable enough to gradually increase speed.

It requires concentration to read quickly. If you don't understand what you read, you will not remember it easily. If

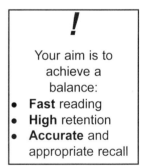

Your aim is to achieve a balance:
- **Fast** reading
- **High** retention
- **Accurate** and appropriate recall

this happens, your concentration will fade. That is likely to lead you to become bored and disappointed.

Metronome Pacing:

Invest in an inexpensive electronic metronome from a music store.

☐ Set the metronome at slow.
☐ Read one line per "tick".
☐ Every half page or so, increase the pace of the metronome by one beat per minute until you reach the fastest speed on the metronome.
☐ Do this for two minutes.
☐ Relax for five minutes.

The metronome will reach a speed at which you will not be able to read every word. This "pushes" your eye and your brain to absorb more than one word at a time without sub-vocalising. This stretches your ability. When you sense that you cannot take in what you read, maintain that speed. Make sure that even though you may not take in the con-tent, you see and recognise (but not say) every word.

Imagine driving on a motor-way at 70 miles per hour. As you approach a town you reduce your speed to what feels like 30. You might think you are travelling at 30 until the police stop you for travel-ling at 40 or 50 - much faster than you thought.

To drive at speed or to read at speed, you must focus your concentration.

PART 5

Eyes and other vitals

Treat your eyes

Eyes need rest and relaxation as much as they need exercise. Reading is easier and more enjoyable when your eyes are relaxed

The muscles that control the eyes are small. They need to be exercised carefully. The following will help you exercise the eye as well as relax them.

Blink:

If you do not blink, your eyes will become dry. Blink often to lubricate them. Put a little note below your screen to remind you to blink while reading from a PC monitor.

> **!**
>
> **Sunning:**
> Close your eyes and face the sun. This helps get rid of tiredness and any grittiness in your eyes. *Never* look at the sun with your eyes open either directly or in a mirror.

Palm:

Rub your hands together for a few moments. When the hands are warm, close your eyes and cover them with your hands. Make sure no light gets in. Hold your palms there for about two minutes.

Workout:

Look straight ahead, then look up as far as you can, then down as far as you can, then to the left, then to the right. Then, look to the top left corner of your visual field, the top right, the bottom right and the bottom left. Hold each gaze for only a couple of seconds. Relax. Gently squeeze your eyes shut then repeat the exercise. After you finish, palm for two minutes.

Read from a monitor
Font size:

For many people, Serif fonts

are easier and quicker to read on paper. Most websites however are changing to small Sans Serif fonts. Decide which you prefer. (The main text of this book is written in a Serif font. The boxes on the side are in Sans Serif.)

Speed:
When reading from a monitor, try using the "down arrow" instead of "page down". Fix your eyes on the last/second last line of the text and move the text up the monitor line at a time using the bottom of the screen as your guide. If the document is long, it may be quicker to read if you print it out. Experiment to find which you prefer.

Light:
Daylight is best. In artificial light, there should not be too much contrast between the light under which you work

> **!**
> Most distractions will be eliminated if you can make the *decision* to take time to read.

and the rest of the room. The main source of light should come over the shoulder opposite your writing hand.

Distractions and Solutions

Improve Concentration:

1. Know your purpose.
2. Use a guide, especially if you are tired or if the material is challenging.
3. Make notes as you read.
4. To help maintain concentration, take a break every 30 minutes for approximately 5 minutes.

Mental distraction:

Mental distraction can happen if you have not made the decision to spend the time on a particular task to the exclusion of all other priorities. Before you begin a reading session, commit to a specific length of time for it. Stick to the time.

Vocabulary:

The better your vocabulary, the faster your reading. To improve comprehension, underline unfamiliar words during Step 3 (Language). Look up the words at the end of the paragraph, page, or section as appropriate.

PART 6
What next?

The only part of the smart reading strategy that requires a little practice is the "speed-reading" (reading more words at a time). Take a few minutes each day to read as fast as you can. Use a guide. Push to increase your reading rate each day. Progress comes quickly after you break the habit of reading with your ears.

The five-step system "chunks down" the task so that you never need to read for more than 30 minutes without a break. Even reading, complicated, technical or apparently 'dry' material, will be a pleasure because the information will mean more to you.

!

You don't have to set aside hours to practice speed-reading, just do it!

If you view reading as tedious, focus and concentration will suffer. If you think of it as interesting or valuable, concentration, comprehension and recall will improve.

Get your Updates!!

Keep speed-reading strategies up to date via email.
1. Visit:
   www.TinaKonstant.com
2. Click "Ultimate Speed-reading Updates"
3. Submit:
   - Email address
   - Name
   - Password:
     informationage
     One word. All lower case.

You will receive FREE:
1. Regular updates on speed-reading strategies.
2. The monthly "Practical Intelligence" Info-Brief packed with ideas, strategies and techniques on memory, thinking, learning and speed-reading.

PART 7

An extra 5 Minutes

Reading in the
Real World

Avoid being a Bottle Neck

Having too much to read every day causes pressure at work. If you have more to read than you have time for, the reason might be either:

1. The need to know every-thing or
2. Procrastination

Are you worried that if you don't read everything that crosses your desk you won't be able to do your job or help others do theirs?

"Needing to know everything" is a controlling attitude. It

frustrates colleagues and turns a desk into a bottleneck. Some of the symptoms are:

- ☐ **Apparent urgency:** dealing with something as soon as you receive it no matter what else has to be done or how important it is in comparison to other priorities. If someone gives you a document to read and says, "this is urgent, you must read it now", don't take their word for it. Although it may be urgent according to others, in *your* schedule of priorities it might be second or third. Prioritise your time.
- ☐ **Nobody does it better:** excellent attitude if you want to work every weekend and most holidays. Most people are capable of doing their jobs well.

Think lucky, have faith,
prioritise and delegate.

- **Generosity:** You cannot
always afford to be gener-
ous with your time. The
people giving you some-
thing extra to deal with
may be avoiding doing it
themselves.

**Don't accept anything that
lands on your desk unless
you know:**

- That you are the best per-
son to process the infor-
mation
- Why you should you read
it and
- What you are expected to
do with it.

Procrastination accumulates
excess reading material. Two
causes of procrastination are
fear or lack of interest.
If a task seems challenging
you might choose to do some

other seemingly important things instead of dealing with reality.

The cure is straightforward. Instead of imagining how bad a task might be, determine precisely what it entails. Get the facts. Then chunk the work into do-able pieces. Then do one piece at a time.

If the cause is lack of interest, find something about the task that motivates you. If you can't and if your desk is always full of paperwork or if you just can't be bothered, consider negotiating your job description. Or find a different job!

Information must flow freely in an organisation. Being a bottleneck achieves nothing. You will be surprised how much you can achieve when you share information.

> **!**
> You don't need to know everything - just where to find what you need to know.

Paper Fatigue

When you have so much unread material that you begin to feel you cannot cope, you experience "paper fatigue": a sense of exhaustion when you go near your desk. This has more to do with perception than with reality. The more effectively you prioritise and organise reading, the faster you get through it. New information becomes manageable.

How to prioritise and organise reading?

☐ Put time aside
☐ Do the 5-Step Process on your In-Tray every day.

> ***!***
>
> If you can find NO reason for reading something - don't!

Points to remember

1. Have a clear, definite purpose.
2. Ensure you are comfortable and that you have adequate light.
3. Use a guide.
4. Read actively; *take notes*, write in margins, circle, highlight, underline and mind-map.
5. Use the new information: discuss, teach, write reports...
6. Refer to notes from books you have read previously.
7. Cross-reference ideas. Think of possible links between sources.
8. If you *have to* read a book rather than want to, reflect on your purpose: what will you get if you read it? What will you get if you don't?
9. Read for only 30 minutes

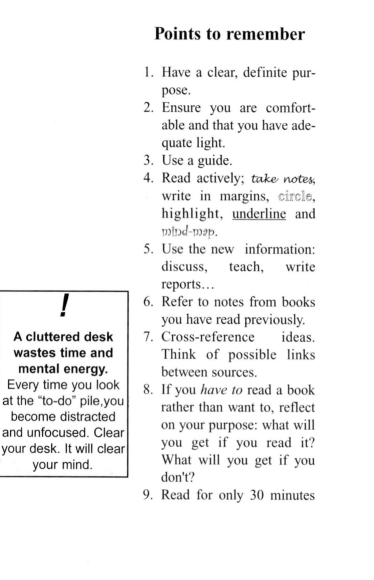

A cluttered desk wastes time and mental energy. Every time you look at the "to-do" pile, you become distracted and unfocused. Clear your desk. It will clear your mind.

at a time. Take a break for five minutes.

10. You will read faster, comprehend what you read and recall the new information easily if you focus and concentrate.

11. Remember: you don't have to read fast all the time. Be flexible.

12. When you encounter a word you don't understand, wait until the end of the page or chapter to look it up unless it stops you understanding the piece.

13. If you use the five-step strategy for novels you'll spoil the ending! When reading novels you can still experiment with different reading speeds.

14. Enjoy the process.

Further reading the 5-Step way

To find books that are ideal for you:

1. Have a clear idea of your outcome and the questions you need answered to achieve it.
2. Visit a good bookshop. Find the section with books that might answers those questions.
3. Based on the information on the front and back cover select books that may be relevant to your purpose.
4. Apply steps one to four of the Five-Step system on each book.
5. From the books that have the relevant information choose which you want to invest in.

UK Book-stores:
Order *"The Ultimate Speed-reading Book"* at any UK book-store

Order online:
For single or bulk orders worldwide visit the "P.I Store" page at:

http://www.TinaKonstant.com

Personalise this book:
Place your company logo on this book and give it as a valuable gift to clients, customers and employees. For more information visit the page titled "A gift they'll thank you for!" at:

http://www.TinaKonstant.com

INDEX

NOTES